six girls without pants

ALSO BY PAISLEY REKDAL

A Crash of Rhinos
The Night my Mother Met Bruce Lee

six girls without pants

poems by

Paisley Rekdal

EASTERN WASHINGTON UNIVERSITY PRESS

SPOKANE, WASHINGTON

Cover design by Scott Poole
Book design by Scott Poole

Library of Congress Cataloging-in-Publication Data

Rekdal, Paisley.
  Six girls without pants : poems / by Paisley Rekdal.
      p. cm.
  ISBN 0-910055-82-3
  I. Title.
PS3568.E54 S59 2002
811'.6--dc21

                                              2002010482

for Catherine Lampman

Contents

wedding me means sure fatality

Ovid, *The Metamorphoses, Book X*

Stupid

In Detroit, a 41- year-old gets stuck and drowns in two feet of water after squeezing his head through a narrow sewer grate to retrieve his car keys.

A joke? Tell me

the story of Job, that book of the pious man
who suffered because the devil wanted to teach God
faith kills through illusion. *Sub*
+ *ferrere* = to carry, to wear boils

like a string of pearls around the neck
and watch son, wealth, house turn
into a sootfall of ash. *Suffer*

the little children I thought was an imperative
not to love but to disdain.
Tell me the one about Santiago Alvarado
who died in Lompoc, having fallen

through the ceiling of the shop
he burgled when the flashlight he carried in his mouth
rammed into his skull.

How Nick Berrena was stabbed to death
by a friend trying to prove a knife couldn't penetrate
the flak vest Berrena wore,
or Daniel Jones dug an eight-foot hole in the sand
whose broad shelf buried him alive.

Hast not thou made an hedge

about him, and about all he hath on every side?
Skin for skin, yea, all that a man hath
he will give for his life.
Tell me what the foolish

should make with their small faith
in roofing, keys just a fingerhold away. This world,
shimmering with strange death in which we know
that to trip on the staircase, wreck the lover's car

is perhaps also to sit covered with ash eating
one's own white heart.

Why doesn't the universe turn a lovelier face to me?

A woman runs to a poison control center
after eating three vaginal inserts while a man
has a cordless phone pulled from his rectum.
I comfort friends

badly, curse the stove for my meal,
live with the wrong man for years.   Faith
for me extends just as far as I'm rewarded; if I laugh
about the mouth foaming with nonoxynol
I'm also awed at the woman's belief propelling her *toward*
not *away from* fear, contrary to skepticism or evidence.

Are there not mockers with me?

and doth not mine eye continue in their provocation?
Bildad begged Job take the smarter path of self-blame:
the sinner must be punished with sin, the stupid destroyed
by stupidity. *Shall the earth be forsaken for thee?* he asked.

How long will ye mock me? Job cried.   God waits
and his words blush furiously up to heaven.

Stupid. Job is stupid for believing.
And I am one of the false mockers chastising
endlessly the faith of one who suffers,
who produces no great thing but shame: to wait

is to destroy the organ and a rash act
must mar this soul. *Stupid,*
how could you love me when everything I give you hurts?

Satan is an old joke to us who don't know

how many temptations lurk
in the commonest household:
the knife, the flashlight. But Santiago knows

and if stealing is the thing that brings one closer

to happiness, and keeping one's hands
free means the difference
between this life and death, that's one line he'll cross.

Few people die intelligently,

the mind gone, shit or urine trickling
between sheets: why not be stabbed
believing yourself protected from the physical indignity
of a knife? *The Lord,*
he destroyeth the perfect and the wicked.

Stupid, listen to me: I'm dying

and everywhere there are azaleas and people speaking French,
so many cups of tea I'll never drink!
Job, you are stupid for your faith as we are stupid for our lack of it,
snickering at the stockbroker jogging off the cliff, though
shouldn't we wonder at all a man can endure
to believe, like this one

whose wife said was so in love
with the world how *could* he look down
while running when he knew
(or should he) all his soul

went up?

What was There to Bring me to Delight But to Love and Be Loved?

I declared, and immediately rejected this. For instance:
a man I loved once liked to hurt women and would tell me
what he did to his lovers. The sight of a woman's slight hips
as she was knocked over a television might give delight. Or the way
bones sounded in skin that bumped or scraped against a wall.
He used to claim he could hear things like this, not
the scratch of a woman's back on a wall, but actual
bone rubbing muscle, skin, joint, the sound
as if sticks rattled in cloth. It frightened him, he said, he found himself
pushing other women to prove he couldn't really hear the sound.
And I loved him. I loved forgiving him. I must admit this
though he never laid a hand on me,
I knew enough about this kind of loss.
There were more significant things
to demand from the world. Such as how
a word could call up more than violence, idea, person, become
reality with only the finest limitations
of meaning. Such as *monster*, perhaps,
or *grave*, or *delicious*. I could say, for instance, that this man
was a *delicious monster* with his strap-colored hair and soft mouth
though where does that place me
in the universe of word? Perhaps you could say *I*
was the monster, searching not for where rivers ran but to the source
of rivers, the frozen nugget of an idea of river: so cold
it almost burns the rock around it. I was the one willing to sacrifice
so many others of my kind; I could listen for hours
to his stories of women whose bones itched within them
and all I could think was *hand, eye, mouth* as if to say the words
was to take his fingers into my mouth, to suck
the warm pink nails between my teeth, or lick the egg taste
from his eye with my tongue. These were more real to me
than the fact he would cry out on the phone or in my bedroom
where we would talk. He would cry and all I could think was
More, let my thighs be another casing for you
if this is the kind of grave you want. I almost thought *grace*. I almost
gave in once but, and this is the truth, he was afraid of me. I
was the coldness of rivers, he said, I was the source
and when he looked down at me lying on the sheets rumpled

4

like ruined skin, he called me his destroyer.

Perhaps the real question in the world is not
what to love, but how to forgive.
What does it take for the monstrous
to be delightful in the eye of God? As if beauty itself
wasn't also obscene—a hand really fleshed claw, a peony
a flowering of blood. Or perhaps a word is really all it signifies, all
we can trust in fact; to name a thing
is to make it so. When I called this man a *man*, you must believe
he became one for me. The source of the river,
not its oceangrasp. What happened to the man I loved
is that eventually he choked a woman almost to death.
We weren't speaking then. Even I, it seems, have my limits.
But I can imagine how he would have told me he could hear her spine
crying out to him, an accusation of the flesh. *What more is there*
but to love like this and to be loved? he asked me once.
You are my source of delight,
an eternal search for grace, I answered. I almost said *the grave*.

Scientific American and St. Theresa: Ecstasy

One foot slips
from its hot cloud. Now bronze-tipped, ready to break
like a criminal into this house of cloth—
a woman—God's arrow
winds up for her heart. From above slap angel's
wings. Gilt brass
spokes that

signal rays where
delight takes up all space. Only the slackness
of her mouth indicates God's
slick mystery lies
within each feather tip, the cross-hatched
carving of marble fog. Her head tilts.
But this one

foot dug
into the swathe of alabaster breaks
like a bone from the rest of the vision.
Only Theresa's face
and left arm dangling down
as if all nerves had been
severed, her will

abandoned,
ignores our logical world.
She is that precise meeting
of God
and a ribcage.

In the gallery I find myself
turning from her, sick of the same elbow's
skidding into mist, her bland

head's similar,
excited tip up, over, out.
For this love
of tongue

and kneecap I,
too, have pooled up into
the dim basin of a skirt,
there—shadowed in
marble—forgetting the female orgasm
was believed a mystery
inclined to wrong-

headedness.
"There is no feeling more pleasant, no
drug," Edmund Wilson says
in my science
magazine, "more addictive than
setting foot on virgin
soil." The cover

has a black-and-
white photo of a 90 year-old
farmer working her field. I see
her eyes shut too,
her head lolls against her shoulder,
making her resemble the Avilan
saint herself

in her toothless
grin. Part gasp, part terror
and delight. "How has technology
changed," her
photographer asked,
"since you were five?"
Perhaps

it is this memory,
inexpressible since so deeply ingrained,
which wrinkles her hands
atop the hoe,

stills even her dress with its negative-
                colored pattern of wheat and dark grass
                                snapping beneath

        the gown's belt,
freezes her kerchief face-framing as a wimple.
        What should I suppose translated
                        this flash
        of joy, this ecstasy
                into such a vessel?
                        The photographer,

        I can imagine,
thinks it's microwaves. A dishwasher.
        There is no fixed point
                        in the universe,
        he could have told her
                        though this is perhaps
                                no more

        startling
than the scab of the first wound in childhood,
        scallops in her black
                        Spanish shawl,
        the noon at the shed door
                                in the arms

        of the one
who loved her. Which science should invent her?
        She's seen the way men rise
                        after a girl
        like a dark cream or hallelujah
                as she passes.
                        You are the first

        and the last,
the Alpha and the Omega might be a phrase
        that barely penetrated the molded skirt
                        of Theresa who,
        unknown to her sculptor, did see a beginning

and end in the language of seasons,
this foot

of her altar done
up like a bed on which all want rests,
all things unknown might yet be
revealed. Things come
together and apart, such saints and farmers
know, choice celebrants
of the intangible:

our heaven
and earth's mineral confessions. The farmer's
foot slips. Theresa's mouth
parts. They are dead
now, both women. From above
there is only

the cherub's
steel shield and arrow, the lens
in which we could believe exists a better life
than ours.
We can look at the evidence
if we like.

We can believe
it all has something to do with joy.

Parable

It was the fourth date, the eighth time
we made love in the Victorian
hotel with its red, skinned carpet and torn sheets,
and you were on top of me again: your chest
glued to mine, our wrists and damp fingertips
aching when the screams began.
It was one a.m. At first the woman
seemed to be a floor below us, then
just across in the apartment
building shoved to within a foot of our
veiled window, her voice a cat's insane
clawing at the sack. *Alone!* she screamed. *Leave me
alone!* She continued so long
we could see her vocal chords
thin to a single red band thrumming in the dark,
the lining of her throat rubbed away with shards
of glass, or gravel. *Alone!* We lay still, one
inside the other as we whispered
words like *the police*, and
a beating, until we realized from the silence
that followed she *was* alone:
her terror, this night, would never be done.

You called the desk clerk. I
pressed my face to the window
to peer down the several brick flights to where
a dim light burned to sift out shapes,
particulars, and then we must
have forgotten it. We slept, and I know we made
love again, several more times again,
beyond orgasm or need, a bodied friction
smacking the pleasure right out of ourselves.
We fucked right through the woman's screaming, eager
from the long divorces and insecurities, too many
years of sexless nights, so that the dull slap
of thigh and finger became a beat with which
we'd rule her out. We'd use hammer and anvil,
wall her up like a victim in a story by Poe

whose rasping, routine cough is the only thing
left after the last brick has settled:
relentless, fixed, true as a clock.

                                                  Last night,
new sheets tucked up almost to our ears, I
contemplated this again, breathed it
from imagination to a figure frozen
outside our open window, a silent gaze
now, since our nights are silent too. Though
there was a moment last week, when,
atop you, I thought of mentioning it again
as a face fluttered into place over yours,
or mine, or both our faces: a glance
of the young man carting groceries out
to his orange pickup, a woman serving coffee
in a cafe downtown. Your hands pushed
along my lower back, pressing me in
and down so that I couldn't breathe
but had to fight against your chest,
fingers digging into sternum as I reared
away. The woman's voice echoed in my head.
Alone! it screamed. *Alone!* And then the face:
heavy jaw, light brows, wide nose. *Whose is that?*
I thought, watching the moon lurch by our open window.
The water of our faces rippled, changed
in the broken lamplight, as the wood of our old bed
struck the night table, and groaned.

Anniversary Song

Look at us there on the museum steps, giggling before the Asian
stone camels and God! The strangers my mother invited to our reception

in photographs spit bubbles out of yellow plastic hoops,
soap suds dive-bombing our knee-length chiffons.

If I'd known then what I don't give a hoot about now—
that even the bridesmaids might have preferred to hurl

invectives or Silly Putty at the guests than blush kisses
against our relatives' damp cheeks, that half the drunken

wedding party would later threaten to kill themselves or divorce—
perhaps we wouldn't have allowed ourselves

to be paraded this way. Who were we to be so happy
among our depressed, gay, single friends?

Look: I'm the cloud of cut-rate polyblend champagne
silk flailing in the marble statue of a tire.

You're the slightly more expensive suit hauling me back out.
Woman overboard! What we did for photographs

we also did for love: mugged till our webbed eyes crossed,
taped condoms to cars under whipped cream and pink crepe studs

to fool the gods of fertility. That's the sort of formality
attached to a wedding. *A weeding*

out of the miserable from the less miserable,
as my aunts murmured in the john.

Guess what? Even now, one year later,
we're the less miserable,

grinning at each other like cannibals over the take-out
and new china, slapping each other on the back, chortling

with self-congratulation. Love!
We're still in love! HA HA HA HA!

Look at us giggling in this photograph, side by side astride
the museum's stone camels in our too-tight wedding clothes,

fat whipping under our arms
as we wave, screaming over our fragile luck

in front of God, the gay, and everybody.

25% Pressure

"Of course I support
        women's rights," he
                declared, "along with those

of the criminally
        insane." His lower
                lip trembled, a slug

of red, the vegetarian
        hands looking screwed
                into their wrist sockets.

He didn't mean this
        as a joke. This
                was political earnestness

before women intent
        on teasing him
                at a party—drift of starlings,

our sexual interest
        like a seatide of foam.
                There is nothing worse

to a man than a woman's
        laughter I read once,
                the year my grandmother

bought me the pamphlets
        on rape. A child
                I read with fascination

the story of a teenager
        whose date suddenly
                pressed her hand

against his jean's crotch,
        then worked her own
                jeans off, forcing her

to lie back
        on the vinyl seat
                that smelled of cigarettes

and breath freshener.
        And I will always remember
                what she wrote next:

Suddenly his penis
        pushed aside my panties
                and he was in me.

Then the quote
        about a woman's laughter,
                its implicit punishment,

its revenge,
        like my revenge
                at this stranger and his lack

of humor. I should say
        he also admitted
                he'd been "pushed aside"

from his job
        when the manager,
                a woman, had reached

for a piece of paper
        and touched his groin
                instead. Pressed it,

actually, he said,
        with full
                "25 percent pressure."

As if to demonstrate
        what deliberateness
                felt like he struggled

toward my leg
      and turned his palm
            sideways so that the branching

knuckles, string
      of fat pearls,
            might stroke the skin.

Then thought better
      of it, withdrew
            seeing my eyes fill

with the red light
      of laughter.
            "Don't do that

without—" he began.
      Then he pulled away.
            When I read the account

of the rape
      the first thing I learned
            to believe in was the accident

inherent to sex,
      the pressure
            of thumb or mouth or penis

to act as if knowing
      more than the mind would,
            seeing more than any eye.

I think this man
      felt that too, hating
            the meats and bloods

and shames of him,
      cloistered
            behind a wall of rectitudes.

When he raised his hand
      up to my leg, hovering

                    past knee as if to touch

the groin, he stopped
          at the place only ruinors,
                    destroyers, numbly

would-be lovers
          would take. He stopped
                    and did not push

past that scrim
          of self-doubt,
                    refused to invite despair in

for something simple
          ruined forever.
                    What does he know

about his manhood
          but that it might be
                    ashamed?

What do I remember
          of the girl in the story?
                    The moments before she was raped

she had kissed the boy,
          had leaned up blushing
                    to finger his shirt

buttons,
          and laughed, gently,
                    in his face.

Caravaggio, My Left Breast and the Time my Mother Took a Wrong Turn in Search of a Children's Halloween Party

It was an accident.

She must have turned
        quite the wrong way down the street
from where the costumed children stamped

beside the line of parents smoking
        in the dark. Not toward where
actors lingered in grease paint, rubber, fiberglass
        fur matted with blood. No,

she turned
        towards the warehouses
and then we saw them, the prismatic

line of men dressed as girls from the warehouse's
        lowest orders. There was the boy with his face
caked, ruined Caravaggio, bleeding into a doorway.
        What could I have made of this?
I thought it was a play. There
        the same lipsticks thickening in the night breeze

and the face paints—at first
        translucent as any window—dulled

onto the canvas of a body whose priming
        was much less
resistible.

                    Caravaggio

painted boys
        with their cloaks half opened, signaling

availability in ways I later learned by rote.
        On the corner,
I saw a man's hand reach for another man's breasts—

a blonde's,
        her huge chest like two small animals
feeding off her. "We're here!" I cried: womanhood
        at a second's threshold.
"We're *not* here," my mother replied
        and turned to ignore

the naked shoulder, the Caravaggio

willingness—desire in chiaroscuro
        with grapes and a bag of ice—the ink-
drawn eyes that from a distance made the face
        look punched in with a pencil.

                We were not here

and we would remain not here, the car
        hurtling on into the night, seeking
someplace else, somewhere else, the arms

        of another stranger's party.

I'm thinking of this now

after a stranger on the train has touched my breast,
        guileless in seeming but not accident—
he'd used my book to grow
        familiar.   "What's

this?" he'd asked, dragging his finger
        down a page-length of text.
Of course I walked away. Of course I'm not bragging

        when I say this has happened before;

that it was simply the nether of me he wanted, the tethered
        parts of me high-strung in their zippers and laces.

Parts I wished myself out of when I saw
        my first Caravaggio, the young Bacchus with his hair

full of grapes and thought *This*
        might be what it is like to feel desire.
And I remember

        not being shocked to discover the boy was indeed
the painter's lover, though I was surprised

to realize I liked what a man liked, that our eyes
        could be so similar. And then I thought
about the prostitutes, the boy ones, the man ones, not
        under glass or paint or cover but real and out
on a street the way my mother or I might be,

walking at night, lips and eyes iridescent
        as flies' wings.
Only now do I know what occasions

might have followed: the kiss or hit or stroke, the roughness
        some use to wrestle with their partners—
the hair come loose, dress torn and stubble
        glowing in the armpit. Or perhaps an elaborate
gentleness to pretend there's difference

        where none really exists. For a minute

in the car I wanted to be the kind of woman
        a man would be
or crave, the gestures of kisses exaggerated
        in layers like a fish skin, like

Caravaggio's nude whose chest was the color of
        fur. No, the color of fruit, hair, hoof, iris.
I remember the delicacy
        of his cock, reclining, shrimp-pink. Half of him
retiring into darkness, the other into light.

        He pouts and stares out at me

and I pout and stare out at him
        whose hand has retreated from my breast in its sad,

slithering gesture.   I walk

to where the women sleep on the train, clutching bags
            of vegetables to them, children tumbling over the shopping
in neat piles around their ankles. I sit
            far away from this stranger
and think of how my breast has attached itself

to me, its fatty mouth suctioned to my heart, the nipple
            where the rest of the animal
has broken off, its slender neck
            burnished, over time, into wound.

I think of Caravaggio
            and what a man's desire looks like
to a woman. On this train, I could look to this stranger,
            past him, where night seeps over a shoulder
like the background of a canvas.
            And I could touch

the grape-dark of his mouth, the hardness of his teeth,
            and then the breast
whose silk is so like a girl's
            there is no point for distinction.

Its muscled roundness can be read like a book

with no words.
            On this page you must point to what you want.
That one with his shoulder
            bared, that one bleeding from the mouth.
The one who quivers and runs away.

Or who reaches for you, willing,

                        then slides back again
into dark.

Six Girls Without Pants

There is enough to warn us. Like this one

in the waiting room with its drapes pinned
as two blue lids. Her head is stapled
and all the fingers crushed,
the nails like drupelets in a blackberry.

I work with those arriving first,
fleshing out forms
with inked-in detail: which muscles look slackened, broke
in the lime-colored light; just evidence
enough to indicate love

was this woman's mortal sport and safety

merely skimmed the surface.
Like the time five girlfriends and I drove
into Tennessee to look for waterfalls
and came upon the Klansmen rattling change
for library funds in coffee cans instead.
Around them? Tender grasses, fields
blushing with wildflowers in red and yellow.

There is nothing to be afraid of

if it is only anecdote.
Not here, where the wild, unnatural
smoke from mufflers wafted through open windows
around our six throats; the waiting, the danger
cloaked in pristine sheets sweet lovers
might once have tumbled in.

Not at the falls where we fought

through water so insistent
the rush gagged our opened mouths
as we swam to the wet tree notched

in granite to our right.

We were merely six girls struggling
toward the surface
when our toes touched something sharp.

We'd tucked earrings, keys, credit cards in shoes,
left our pants on the shore so water wouldn't
suck us down. We'd drive back

in wet t-shirts and underwear to dry,
our thighs dipped in sunlight
on the car seats. High up in the truck,
no one could look down at us
and see. We joked

about this nakedness
all the way back to the city. This invisible,
this ridiculous,

vulnerability.

F i n i s h e r

Delos carves its few lines, dissecting
sea from sky where the Aegean's shoreline,
once called *wine dark,* has turned

azure, cobalt, white, so bright the sky's
color seems worn in comparison. Massive herms,
their marbled heads lopped off

at the cocks' stiff bases, gleam. What's great
is the every nuance of erection
carved at the lingering

base: the tightening of stone
vein and muscle,
the strain as the invisible

penises rear from their block constraints
and beckon in our imagination. The way one Greek
on the tour boat cried *Delphi!* into the transparent

wake erupting past helm, and the dolphin
rose up like myth we must rework
as truth each time it's witnessed. This island is

full of rumors, unfinished
lines and headless gods,
mosaics patterning off into ellipses

of black and white. In the fragmented
dark of the temple you can barely see
the scarlet tongue, olive coil of the great

serpent that pursued the twins' mother here.
Here, where Zeus' mistress must,
rushed into pregnancy, have felt

incomplete, not done
with her infatuation. *His great knees,*
fistful of gold. Like the American in dark

glasses who loudly confided in us
tales of her years in the circus,
who couldn't see any *stop*

as her stories grew stranger with suicides,
mutual disappearances. She's insulted
the Canadian already, telling her, *It's not*

as if your country is different.
Why sew that fig leaf on your purse? As if
all borders were irrational.

Don't you see the penis? Look,
even the crude outline of the crane carved
into the herm's man-height slab

of marble suggests the truth
someone cut off. The lines
of dismantling are too clean

for time, too sure,
and the black ground lacks evidence
of gradual dismissal.

Nor can you see,
from the island's highest point, Naxos
due to smog that blushes

plum against sea, violet
smoking as the horizon diminishes.
No mother's terrible journey pursued

as partridge, hawk, fox,
and finally snake, all on the verge
of giving up. Did I mention

that on the boat ride the American
took her glasses off and suddenly we could see
the truth? She was terrified,

and the facts of her life evaporated in faith
like smoke before us. She stands now

before the herms one older couple

can't stop having their picture
taken in front of: the lidless sky,
marbled paleness sizzling in the distance.

They look out onto this craftless sea,
the port tinged gray and coral pink.
Their white hair, like haloes, frames them.

Look: now the wife glances up
to the cobalt sky
as if she's heard a rumor.

The camera shutter snaps
at the masculine stems
and already it seems, even to us,

she's disappeared.

Wood/Cut: Two Japanese Prints

I. "Geisha Dressing," anonymous
History, Legend, Myth

In this antique print she slinks and dreams in her edged
keyhole with a fist of hair and with her comb
threatening from the mouth like another mouth,

the black lozenge of a mirror obstructing
our view into her body's unknown:
a saffron underworld. Her belly puckers

with the bend of one arm wrenching
back, pinioning some object
invisible to us as her kneecaps

or bed roll. Naked.
Her nipples are the shape of pink
corn kernels. Her yukata is blue.

No *kiwame* would have prevented us
this glance, this cherry blossom branch firmly
laddering up wall side revealing no man but

happier nights awaited with teeth.
No censor would have imagined her
living out of this flat surface, this nothing

landscape floating on cherry wood
and cherry flower which the cut
itself implies with its lack of perspective.

She is our courtesan.
From far away the thickened, man-like arms
look strong enough to break her own frame. Now

we're moving closer and see the fine brow hair
starkly etched like possum fur, the edges
between her daggered teeth stamped into the paper, and,

like this, we can see the artist's
designed her to seem
part animal, part elegance.

II. "Tale of a 1000 Condoms/Geisha & Skeleton," Masami Teraoka
Trades & Occupations

They need three artists for the work:
sketcher, carver, printshop master.
Color they'll fill

in by hand, red
leaded *tan-e* and pink *beni-e*
safflower fleshing an auroral

landscape. "Pictures
from the Floating World" they called them,
by the Buddhist term referring

both to territories in Tokyo
and to the blocks themselves,
hovering between black outlines lacquered

into mulberry, liquid patternings of color
settled one by one like birds
coming home to roost.

"The Floating World":
this transference between life
and almost life signified

by fingernails of cherry blossoms raining
against panes of the kabuki theatre,
the slender wood rising of the bridge a farmer crosses,

his blue-black smock dotted with white
reminders of a better life, better time.
Now snow flurries

as the geisha tears condom
wrappers open
with her mouth while the skeleton's arm reaches for her,

a claw from the jewel-toned backdrop
of spattered fire. Feathers
erupt from her hair. And again, bunches of white

and peach petals, their velvet
adhesive to the skin
of this model scarred by sores badly painted over.

She chews her hair
as the condom pops
from its enormous envelope.

Trades and occupations.
In the museum, examining this
print, I recall my piano teacher

who kept an honest metronome
constantly at work
that gave us outline, rhythm

between which we could slide in
color and tone,
the black mathematics of adolescence

ticking us into form.
I pouted
while her son lay in another room, dying

of a new disease and wanting
to tell me off for her, overworked
with his medication, as I clambered

round the keys.
In later times, I read, Japanese
artists beat metal for flakes to add to print

backgrounds: glinting gems
microbe-size they mixed with glue and gauffraged
by rubbing the blocks together.

The result was shimmer, mirage,
a gleam that resembled gold or silver
and made the embossed surface look glossed.

My teacher's son was an architect who had designed
the most beautiful building in Singapore.
Now he was sick. Now there was that flicker,

that gleam as I had seen it, a keyhole
into adult life going on past the living
room, kitchen, the hall's silvery water

marks. Some real suffering floated
in this architect who stood at the end of plague
literature scholars newly murmured about. Watch:

the fat white foot of the geisha grinds
a torn packet into the ground. "Tale
of a Thousand Condoms/Geisha And Skeleton"

is Teraoka's title and if he chose
his models with purpose, notice
no men are dying here but women: architects

of ancient art spied through
back alley curtains and wine cups, their poetry
the nape of neck, bow arch translated

into the spit, come, blood, and snot of us:
the black gum edge of language, thus history
scrawled like arterial lines, ticker

of the heart tossed in the background.
He kept their animalness, too, the wrench
and gasp of my own geisha's portrait.

But now her sensuality suggests
the death tremor, perhaps the feral
glissando of leaving one's body.

Light exhausts you,
my teacher's son said, *too bright
and huge for words,*

laying like cement against the skin. So off
lay that distance he wrestled into while I banged
thoughtlessly away, complaining

of nothing to wrestle against,
not this silk, not this black weight
of a hairstyle combed a thousand times,

the press of the restrictive kimono heavy
as the bed sheets tucked
to keep the son's sick torso

down. And these women
tearing their way out of their cloth
sacks, their obis and netsukes?

The skeleton beckons
and this one relents. Her clenched fingers
slide to where his pelvic bone

angles in the repose
of mortality. But her motion
misleads. Rather than a gesture

of offering, the woman's hand pushes
away, her condom's disk no
sexual invite but saint's medallion.

Both sword and protection.
Between them a tiny,
insubstantial shield.

III. Actor Prints

You can see it along the museum's corridors: saint,
animal, sex. Perhaps I should turn away
watching women

pose like this, by the fact
we are the only ones

watched. I peep into the painted keyhole

and see no love scene between man
and man, no revelation
of two people sitting, eating, but

a woman at her bath. Is this all we can imagine
of a private life? I like to look at myself
in the mirror, my head between the border-

lines of its frame; molded
into contained space.
Femininity is an open mouth, I've read.

And heard desire unchecked
could kill through it, and seen the similarity
in movements mocked between woman and man:

the lipstick, crossed legs, shoulderpads.
"Ten years more," Hokusai once said,
"and I might become a great artist."

He meant, perhaps, the mastery
of artifice that demands attention
to transference. More veil,

more silk, more liquid
priming for the face to take on shared
architectures of a self. I too need these

strange conjunctions, uneasy
alliances.
Didn't Hokusai draw the woman

and the octopus? Erotic
cuts of couples leaning face to face, face
to back, bottom to top?

He would have printed up the drag
singer too, I think, just as he did the women together
in the public bath, the man's eye

spying on them, taking notes.
He might have made a cut

of me, a woman in a dead man's tuxedo

bought with its left leg higher
than the right and its satiny lapels I cannot seem
to open wide enough to indicate the curve

of my chest, thus my allegiances. Cuts
against the grain
that reveal a similarity of purpose:

the doe with her rack of antlers, peahen
preening blue and dusty gold with a thousand eyes
to look upon herself.

Ten years more
I might be dead. So examine me now, this paint
mask with its exact placement and stitching

that strains against sharp
brow bone, the clothes
that fit me better than a coffin.

I put them on,
I am the Japanese woman
in the keyhole, the geisha before the skeleton,

the dying son watched.
I go home, I am nothing.
So I leave you with them. I take them

off.

IV. Festivals & Pageants

The American Secretary of State and Secretary
of Defense sit
on a red stage mounted by students

screaming on television about Iraq's
political innocent.

Another invasion. The results of it

revealed daily through video scrim,
like these live debates
I listen to from Midwestern colleges.

Today the students' arguments are left
as background music
to my cosmetic preparation; only

deep chords of frustration register.
I find myself
agreeing to something

I haven't fully heard.
Outside the neighbor's cat
has gone into heat; she howls

continuously for an attention
no one's giving her.
The birds are sexual even,

and chase each other in rough flight
round the tree so that anyone who passes
must duck, must raise a hand before the face

as if saluting the violence
of sex itself. The thing
making the rational irrational

and the irrational
mad. You know the type:
"...living only for the moment, turning

our full attention to the pleasures
of the moon, of the cherry
blossoms and maple leaves;

not caring a whit for the sadness
staring us in the face, refusing
to be disheartened—"? These are the layers

of a preparation. First, the powdery,

desert-colored base;
the eyeliner, then gloss. Blush,

to make the face look heated
in arousal.
Thickened, dark lips signal

the swelling of the vaginal
sheath: a readiness
for engagement. Then the animal

jewels for ears, sapphire eyes winking
from the darkness of hair.
The lashes must look barbed

or spiked. But before all this comes
the porous, blue-white
paste to cover the face. A paint,

a bluing.
I put it on, take it off,
strip and slither

out of pants and camisole top.
"Like a gourd floating on the river
current, this

is what we call the floating world,"
Ryoi wrote of the spring festival.
The television screeches

as my blue mask bubbles
under water, runs
like a dog's rabid slather over chin

and throat. I marvel
in the shower over muscles'
flex and beckon, the skin still taut, the shoulder

still shaped. Scrape away any blackness
pebbling a femininity.
Scrub my face, my back

and listen to the cries of birds
and water, the cat's inconsolate mewing.
For a moment, they drown

out the television audience's applause;
the sound of my own, tuneless
humming. "Singing songs,

drinking wine, not caring at all
but floating, floating," Ryoi wrote.
This simplest art

on the verge of war.

Death and the Maiden

after the paintings by Hans Baldung, 1517

The Painter
Death cups her to him and his fingers spread
like a web rotting to dust, strung between
the archway of her breasts. Look how her red
lips slightly part under his teeth: her plea
goes unheard by God as the fleshless fingers
twist in her side. Age entered into Eve
this way, through gates of mouth, and hand, and hunger.
Now youth rises like a flight of birds eased
from fields or loosened by a farmer's scythe
in harvest-time. Her arms are smooth and white.
She's beautiful. I've sometimes dreamt of her, her sighs
digging in my mouth, hands reaching from behind
to clasp my back and thighs to her rounded womb.
I wake, choking. *Her body*, I think. *Become a tomb—*

The Maiden
My mother kissed me on the brow: "Aren't you
the lucky one for youth?" Our peat cart moaned
in transit, slowed by her thin fist struck through
with light. Our horse pranced, the wood wheels rolled
among the autumn leaves as peat squares passed
like empty mouths to the hands of customers.
"Consider now the bones and flesh amassed,"
she whispered, "like treasures for the wind." That year
she'd die, and what was I without comfort's uses?
From this thought came the love of love, the body
as a free thing. I make no excuses.
I passed myself like bracelets to an army
of suitors who shared my skin for a pelt.
Go ahead: use me up. I'm an empty mouth myself.

Epithalamium

Excerpts from the myth of Atalanta and Hippomenes, based on the drawings and tapestry painting by Noel Hallé.

Atalanta held her bow
in her left hand. And her beguiling face
was, for a girl, quite boyish; for a boy
it had a girlish cast—one could have said.

Ovid, *The Metamorphoses*, Book VII

This is it. The phrase my record album of myths began and ended with, the start of the tale of Atalanta and her two lovers. Its cover bore a French painting of her racing with Hippomenes. I stared intently at it as a child, turning the cardboard sleeve over in my hands—the girl half-boy, the boy half-girl—as an actress repeated her tale about a princess of questionable upbringing whose first lover was killed by his mother. About a second who proved treacherous in a race. About the vanity of female error.

Atalanta offended everyone, the actress mournfully warned. *Father, suitors, goddesses, uncles, turned from bear-girl to lioness, unsexed herself forever after a dalliance in Venus' temple.* Even as a child there was something wonderful about this. There was something gorgeous about the flow of disaster into other disasters: seeds sprouting into newer seeds, a painting unfolding itself into little squares of color, light. The needle popped and spun in its grooves as I listened, unfolding image and character that extended into whatever of myself I imagined brand new. When it was through I could not be satisfied except to listen to it again. I'd place the crystal-headed arm back at the black beginning, the edge where chaos hissed, too smooth to speak by half, until its equilibrium

was punctuated and a Delphic voice
jumped through the grooves. I listened
and heard again a woman speak words I
was too timid to read but memorized
the way air is memorized by lungs:

Sing with me, muse.
Now I am ready to tell the story of how bodies changed
into other bodies.

I sometimes wish

objects could free themselves from meaning,
so that a tree would be
a tree and not also a painting
of it, become
the positive not negative
silhouette; but this

is what Hallé shows me is impossible.
*Love is not love when it is stone and whispers
its own secrets apart from us,* he says.

What does it mean to be a single thing?

Hallé pauses. Before him
a boy skips forward, left leg kicking. And a girl
soldiers after him, holding her aching side with a hand.
Thoughtlessly, she reaches for the apple
rolling to her feet.

She thinks she wants it
because in it she sees herself.
She thinks it is herself

because it is how she wants to be seen.

fig. 8 study of atalanta and hippomenes' left arm

same reach, same dumb finger twisted under middle
digit, thumb lower beak of the pelican, a gaping wish
in black and white ellipses. Lines here are clear if slightly
rumpled with shadow, the squat and beaky thumb
possessing the only lightness with its nail: one blind
eye, one tooth, one horn window through which to see
the world. His hand reaches. Below it, fog
as outline of Atalanta. Her heavy haunch pulls back:
deer's flank, a satyr's thick leg. Back and forth,
pause and pull ahead. Exquisite. Sexless. Now dance.

Enter the first boy.

A Love Story: Atalanta meets Meleager

He wanted to give it, gift it. Skin. Meleager, Althea's son, who'd had Atalanta long in mind from meeting on hillsides, she raised by bears after being abandoned by her father. He called her his Artemis. Jealous, the moon twin scooped a fist of mud, shaped a boar and sent it spinning to Calydon. To kill it, Meleager invited all Greece's heroes to a hunt. In myth, we wouldn't know Atalanta without this invitation. She arrives formed whole and solitary, loved but as yet unloving; a history hinted at in rough lines and bearish attitude. Meleager watched. "If she rides with us like a man," his uncles complained, "sit here for her and spin; a man grown girl is worth a woman weaponed." In myth Atalanta makes the first successful strike. Blood bristles below the boar's ear, the shaft grinds against jaw bone. Moved by shame, men crowd round the black form, panting, terrified. Imagine how it wheels and stabs Ancreus deep in the groin, traps Atalanta behind its right flank, staring at the gold eye alternately fixing her then gazing blank, glazed with its own pain. What does she see? *A little fruit a little while is ours, and the worm finds it soon.* She will die, just as Meleager who kills the boar, guts it with one fast jab through its ribs. Meleager who, upon presenting her tusk and skin, will kill his uncles snatching back the prize to offend her. Atalanta is, yes, going to die, is going to love again even after Meleager whose mother takes the

Capitulation   came from rage. I took

this boy in the woods   finding fight sweeter
than any hunt.   Under him canvas

ripped, let skin   fuse to larger,
new bone, striation   of muscle. Salt

whipped   across my mouth, final
as any kiss   pressed to breastbone.

He wheels like a boar.   His foot drips
brimstone, he smokes   as he walks.

"So beautiful," he   insists, copying
my voice: echo   location. We slip into

the same   pool fingering reflections; share
eyes made to see only   each other.

Clinging   to this surface
truth he could waste   to white

lillies at the shore   of my
difference;   this slender double

x my legs and arms make   over
modesties. Not much I must defend

from him   fixed
as any amphora   I could fill myself in,

spill over, twin and   helix within—caveside
and   inlet—promontory of

rock softer   than what bodies make.
Side by side we're   gemini in glass

protective brand the Fates gave her at his birth, and for revenge of her brothers burns it, stirs its cold ashes with a toe. In her first embrace, Meleager dies in Atalanta's arms. What does the eye tell her then? Black skin shrivels against her throat. Boar bristles prick her breast. "I would I had not come", she whispers. From above: fresh snow the color of a moon. And on his face: the ashy smile of what for years she will call love. Good Meleager. Dying—

reflecting us double   *our means*
and size. Give up, give   in, *atoms hiss*

between us   *finding space to share as one,*
the exactness   *of a nothing.*

My hands pull   *out from him,*
release shared heat,   *blood pinks*

warmed to a kind of dawn   *I want to gift*
to him,   *to give it. Skin.*

fig 4 cupid statue on pedestal, upper right hand corner, far right section of painting

Found the gold snake dipped in cream? The little useless
wings shrivel behind marble shoulders, his cheek tipped, cocked,
ready to fire like a gun. A boy with exactly his head
in brown frolics below him (what does the artist mean by
this repetition?). The fat foot swivels on its pallid slab, gold
quiver like a city in miniature by an ankle. There's the ghostly
belly ringed by arm and upper thigh, a mirror above which,
let's see, the index finger ticks singlely on a pale fist. Clocktalker,
a boy about to pick his nose? What's this stone boy
insinuating? *Read my lips*. Love's Big Secret.

You have no need of husbands, the oracle advises. *Shun any marriage. Though you stay alive, you will have lost yourself.* So what? Atalanta declares. *So will,* the oracle sighs. *Doesn't anyone ever listen to me?* Atalanta shrugs, throws down a few gold coins. And yet. To condemn oneself to an idea of loneliness? For years she vacillates: Atalanta, the running girl who could never be satisfied with the choices life gave her. As if the only alternative to solitude was sorrow. As if death itself was a purely feminine failure.

In this tale, Atalanta abandons the hills she raised herself in, makes her way back to a home cursed childless since her father's abandonment. *Now,* he says, *you can get married.* The oracle sends a telegram. *Don't do it.* To compromise, Atalanta devises a plan. On a field of chickory, on a field of bedstraw she'll run. All suitors she can audition by challenging them to race. The losers heads she will collect on stakes.

Death makes us faithful to nothing, Atalanta tells me, though it makes some faithful to self-pity. The idea of loss makes some only want to lose more. Hippomenes arrives, like all new lovers, unaware of this. He simply sees and wants. He simply makes a bargain with Love. *Give me this woman once and I*

will worship every day, he says. And in
the morning apples arrive at his bedside
from Tamasus grove: the richest land in
Cyprus. They shimmer in the light like
women's bracelets. Frightening as blood,
I know, my own gold ring dulled over
time like the point of childhood fables.
Irresistible   to   some   as   coins,
perhaps.   Or   open   cages—

Hippomenes Longs for Her

So beautiful she is an investment! The king's daughter
whispers to the moon, praises it like she was its daughter.

My lute opens its toothless mouth wide as despair.
On the hilltops, in the lapis grasses, I wait for her daughters.

You once asked what I would do for a wife. Just this: cut
her hair, switch doll for spindle, end her days as a daughter.

Gold apples tucked in my tunic. In dreams Love
gave them for a sacrifice. Now I roam Samothrace for a daughter.

The last day I was a child I entered love with eyes white
as river stones, my fingers tracing the face of a farmer's daughter.

It makes no difference how long she refuses me. I'll spoil her with silk,
braid kisses into her hair, grace her with gold like an only daughter.

I know men laugh at my beardless cheeks, my girl's knees. They mock
supposed frailty. Their voices rise when I race: "O, Daughter!"

All sea roads wind to Africa, forgetting Greece. When I go I'll take
only sweet things with me: red honey, black grapes, a daughter.

They ask me my name at the race gate: Hippomenes, fast as Apollo,
son of a poor king. It means Unlucky. It means Horse's daughter.

Last night Love gave me a wooer's charm to conquer brides. Show her
old, show a lover dying. Give her hope for new life: raise a daughter.

A Commission

Noel Hallé, painter, 1711-1781

The nobleman's girl arrives, her skirt filling
up a doorway. Pale with light as the cake
layered like St. Bride's: architecture
mimicking nuptials to be devoured.

Velvet darkens her cheek.
Shadow darkens the velvet.

I take out brush and linger as if to adore

what on canvas must be re-
constructed: the silver
tonality of neckline, mustard
in the bodice braid. As a child
before my mother's table, I'd counted out such

colors of jars in mineral hues, crushed and blown
into hearts, used to transform the angles
of the body with. Apple green, a dust of fine blush
like the covering on damsons.
Rose hollyhock.

Spattered with the peruke's gray sheen,
now in her face, blood struggles
under the girl's mask of arsenic.

It is like watching something living

crawl beneath something dead.
I look at her and think of gods
who clasp nymphs in fountain
statuettes as if they wanted them to drown,

and wish their stone laurels could be stripped away,
the metallic sheen of silk
pulled from shoulders, gilding gone in preference
for the real form of us to stay put
and shine.

If I could I'd draw through the girl

a hardier seed than classical urges trailing off
into pastilles. More permanent
than the painted draperies or foot's arch
curve similar to any aqueduct's.

In my bedclothes later, the girl turns

to a collection of thin papers whispering.
I grip her slim wrists to chain her where she lays
with scarf and pillowcase.

Close my eyes. Imagine

the sheen of her young
body as it rises. Harder without the dress,
I believe. Broader
and strong, her boyish limbs churn and churn

like smoke in this white space between us
of my eternal bed, my need.

**fig 2   study of a dog, circa 1765, black chalk drawing,
finished as lower far left-hand corner of painting**

Flank speaks and desire must follow. Poor boy
driven by his own dumb body. Poor boy stumbling
over cabbage leaves, each ear shaped like a child's
mitten. His raised forepaw has disappeared due to
the artist's indolence. All salt and brownwood, he slithers
by his salmon-colored master ignoring *dogwant* in favor
of voyeurism. The girl's tunic slips. Now a slice
of roseate moon dipped in eclipse just peeks. Poor boy,
getting only this—vision of gold playtoy tossed
his way but never for him. Here's the coolness of mud,
velvet underbrush a livid seaweed green for respite.
All the world's a stone escarpment to be leaped.
All our little berries pinched out, painted nipple pink.

Race: A Medley

'Any girly thing will do: take blue chemise gowns, sheers sprinkled
with hearts and wring from them a face you want. Vendors know

The myth: centuries before poets loved to tell
how the goddess of love gave Hippomenes gold apples from Juno's grove,

the hardest sell to soul's intangible. Love needs more drapery, gold polish, a
familiar thought to hang dumb desire on. Still

a trio meant to distract Atalanta in the race.
But few would say he was young, effeminate, used to

wanting more? Try kinky sex tips culled from
shrink's records, diaries and blue movies; flash them at the world for enticement

always getting his way with girls. You'd think Atalanta was not a woman
to be tempted by frivolities like apples. Grief for Meleager kept her hair

like pearl dust or dove's wings
ground down for a love charm. "She'll want you if

short, her brown arms tough and muscled.
Grief became her so she became the image of her grief.

you want her more," is our advice, thus try
gauze gowns, shirred lilac bodices. Love's big secret being similar to

Her race with Hippomenes was just a way of discouraging the oracled
inevitable: a marriage, a childbed. When love's first apple fell she saw,

war, route the enemy by distracting with small
skirmishes. Dress her in red or black, clear hues

yes, gold first, but then such loveliness glowing in dust... She glared
into her own reflection: high cheekbones, hair shorn and curling.

that bring out tone to your faux wedding night, and strip
back the bed to indicate passion is near. For her: a little perfume behind the ear

Being young, beautiful, she mused how the apple's curve
did not distort but enhanced the structure of face, hue of skin;

will add support. Try some decolleté for pizzazz or bright
jacquards, microfibers for enhanced form,

perhaps she saw herself just once for how she was, how she hoped she'd never
change. Then the second apple. She didn't want

the miracle bra. Change is good for any man.'
Thus spoke Venus.

To stop her race but how lovely the first one was, she must take
this as well. She jogged on, the apple glistened. In it her reflection changed,

Desire she catalogued according to sacrifice, mish-mash,
a shamble of artifice including lace stays, sunsets and greeting cards

distorted itself out of proportion. Old here, weak-breasted, her whole
life threaded out in a palm so she could see the path before her death.

with no one's name. As when the earth itself was shapeless, she loved
anonymity, believing substitution to be its highest compliment: not face, but

It was vanity that struck her now, as Hippomenes inched ahead, her future
a promise of a solitude she couldn't bear. In memory the Cumean Sibyl

forms. All brides she made vague through veil so men couldn't see
what was coming for them; vice-versa. "You can be whatever I make of you," she'd

rocked in a tiny cage. "I want to die," the seer whispered.
Now in her hand she held the last, saw Meleager's face

threaten. Girls who croon for stars or soldiers, marry too young
face an eternal curse of boredom in love. 'Specificity kills lust off, you'll

shrivel in pain, the red tongue blacken. Again. He was dying in her arms
again. She swatted at her cheeks and felt tears

sicken in his arms. Love's interest
is rarely sustainable. No thing maintains its shape for long.' So

stick to her fingers. Venus smirked.

The dull fruit sank in Atalanta's tunic. That's the myth. That's

Venus snapping out pistachio convertible
halter tops, plum blushes, silk faille and ottoman knits lets her divine fog

the truth. But if she told friends later it was desire that made her
stop, sit down, that it was the previously undiscovered

machine roll out pink clouds from which she appears chimera-like wielding arrows
to pierce the most intractable hearts, with lipsticks and mirrors in which

merits of her suitor's ankle that finally broke her, so that she had to turn away
and stare instead at grass, at road, at sky, why dispute the fact

you have never looked better, have never looked
more delicate and alone. 'Choose!' she cries, as, yes, even then,

they had a reasonably happy marriage? That (though cheated) we still could say
she chose? Meleager's face withers in her palm. She hides her pride and shame

your skin seems to collapse in on itself and you are a fruit ripening too quickly,
a beginning and an end, a choice you choose, you must choose

like breasts in a tunic, gold apples. The crowd roars, Hippomenes crosses the line.
Now he turns and smiles. He walks back to collect his prize.

Atalanta paused.

Now I am ready, *she said,* to tell the story
of how bodies changed
into other bodies.

(Like all heroines,
she could not help but think of the future,
how it might faithfully recall her
without once saying her name.)

**fig 23 woods and turbaned head of girl not watching
race, middle section of right panel**

What to look at. Up at dawn, like a prophetess,
while your man wears a gnome's hat and stares
at nothing. Now you in the seer's turban, gold
tongue clipped, wrapped, bound. Blue-green woods
surround: the heart of an emerald which only extremes
of dark and light may penetrate. Your face is road-colored.
The dollop mouth parts, shine evaporates against this
lesser curve of cheek. Below you pants loser
and victor, shimmer of tossed fruit in the possibility
of marriage. How many months it has been since this man
groaned under your fingertip! Now there is the outer edge
of the painting. Now there is the world around you
concentrating on this benediction. But not you, girlfriend.
What do you crave? Edges, dismissals, borderlines.
Firm wood frame, a country full of beginnings.

A Metamorphosis

*She's licking her between the legs. She's raising up two fingers
so as to pinch the other's silky, pouch-like breast with its nipple ring.
A benediction! The camera freezes on their feral grins as the one
with green hair lunges at the one with red. They're dressed as policemen,
carpenters, military officers. She's got her boot in that one's face. She's
licking it between its laces. There is no place they cannot touch
each other, no frame of reference they must abide by: leather
boot or fist, fedora or cowlick. They could be anyone.* Show. Me. *She's sliding
out of her Victorian gown like a moth from its membranous casement.
Now she wants to be rescued. She wants the red-haired soldier
to bite her clitoris. Red and Green, like some disastrous
Christmas packaging. Green behind Red clutches her hipbone,
feeds her popsicles.* Bend over. Strut. Surprise me. *Red lingers in fish-
nets and high heels unwrapping Green from a bone-colored suit.
Chalky popsicle sticks disappear, one by one. It's a race
to see which of the two will give out first,
will parade the other best like a suit of armor
or sacking cloth. She's kissing her on the mouth. She's tying her to a chair.
She's dressing her up in the French maid uniform. Now she's taking it off.
Now they are two men out for an evening
stroll, the slick black tongue of Green's tattoo just flicking
out of her tuxedo collar.* Watch me,
*reads the bubble cartoon from Red's mouth. She's chewing on a knuckle.
She's unbuckled the carpenter's belt. It slides to the floor like a dead body
between them. Her knees are around that one's ears, this one's fist
disappears between that one's legs.* Don't stop. You can't stop.
Tell me, *Green begs. Popsicles the color of her hair slip
from her mouth. Bubbles rise up, a conversation. They're saying. They're begging.
They're praying. They're bound and gagged. They're in school
uniforms and eating doughnuts. Now this one's a train conductor punching
tickets; the other's the recalcitrant tourist. You understand?
A bubble, endstop. Green watches. Red says.* How to. Come to. Love.

"I Was a Teen Geek, Now I Dress Like a Complete Freak": Cross-Dresser on the Venus Hour Show

"Is this some transgender thing

you're going through?" asks the talk show audience. "There's none
      of this where *I*
come from." Which is, I'd say, the point. I'm honest. These spikes
      aren't permanent,
they're super-glued. My white contacts, of course,
      a fake.
Four-inch lashes ferny as undergrowth? Dyed black, purchased
      at a Las Vegas
costumer's. Heels, yes, fishnets and metal chains drape

artfully around this torso I occasionally wish would
      burgeon with new
breasts, slenderize at the waist to a finely tapering point
      a man's hands
could encircle. I've shaved off eyebrows in favor
      of purple curlicues
like smoke that drift past forehead onto my shaved
      pate that must glisten
with sweat in front of these Philistines at the Venus Hour show.

You tell *me* what kind of man I am. I'll complete myself

with earrings, black fingercaps in latex, underthings
      constructed like torture
devices that strap down penis, shave weight from hips and,
      when covered
only by a thin mesh sheath, glow green in dance club
      black light. I'm not a man

to put too fine a point on things, but dress
      is imperative.
Desire is a series of changes. Nature doesn't favor the drab.
      "You look
like a damn spider died on your eyes," a frat boy sneers.

"Do you even like
women?" As if I couldn't! I look into mirrors

to see girls I've loved
          staring me in the face;
pieces of them superimposed, split, transfigured
          larger than life in flawless
display. I sometimes think self-love, for me, actually is a two-way
I can actually finger the cheerleader, my nonexistent prom date, suck and
kiss
          the girl from study hall—

There's not much difference

between the canvas of my body and a *Playboy*. Tell that
          to middle America.
"What kind of boy are you?" the show host growls
          as I recall my mother's
myth of the girl and boy who swapped appearances to pursue
          each other.
"One like you," I whisper. On certain Fridays
          I go out
in dog collars and Chanel with blue pumps whose heel tips
          I've dyed blood red.
If you listen, their clatter's like applause.
          When I walk
they squeal and sigh for me, like girls in love.

fig 16 woman's big toe, lower right section of painting's center

daub of flesh, silver nubbin out of darker silver, cloth, indigo
recess, shadow on shadow.   Potato eye, night's callous.
Little gray newthead rising to a white pitch.   Look as it
swims up from this depthless water: o milk stain, o glaucoma!
Human brightness (*this one point*) under a swathe
of gilded fleur des lis.

The End

Just one time, he begs. Atalanta frowns, but lets him run his hands along her ribcage and lets him ease her spine onto the cool temple marble, settling his weight cautiously on top of her—

It isn't till after that she feels teeth cut into the slick pink skin of her own mouth, her hands yanked suddenly to earth, heavy as if wagon wheels were tied to them. She stumbles after Hippomenes out of Venus' temple to see his naked ass sprout stiff hairs and a quivering tail. *Look!* she cries to cry, but it comes out somewhere between a roar and a squeal. Tracery of smoke-on-smoke. Snifter of light. Mouth open, black gums snapping words that have no meaning anymore. Can you imagine this sort of death perpetual, the eyes of your mate the eyes of the only one who cannot touch you? Hillsides filled with the sharpness of animal fur. And each sexed nerve a singing number of wrongdoing. Cybele flies in, her dark cart ready to be hitched, drawn: black into cream. Yellow into silver. *In the beginning,* the chariot's gold masthead reads. *Some   excruciating   distance.*

The Critic

Denis Diderot 1713-1784

The body in action is the best picture of the human soul.
I write, touching down lines with my feather quill, a pinion
snapped from the eagle in which its flight continues life
in stillness. The canvas is the best way to stop form.

I write, *Touching, these lines. They cloud our opinion*
about the girl running after her suitor. Look how her impatient
stillness blurs on canvas with the stopped shape of a nod.
I think of more such bodies: yesterday's slaughtered market bull,

a farmer whistling, the maid at my table. So impatient,
my wife used to berate me in the sorest manner
at the body of this table, her face black as the market bull
that died with a bubble of dark blood forming at its mouth.

Yes, she used to berate me in the sorest manner.
I take up pen, write: *I actually find myself there*
in Hallé's tableau, its dying sun like a bubble of blood.
I shall remain leaning against this tree, watching this girl,

forever finding myself in the composition
so long as the couple runs. What rare form I'm in.
In dreams I've leaned against this tree, watching this girl.
It seems the painter is helped by my weakness:

the composition goes straight to my soul.
I actually find my wife in the girl's form, myself
the painter weak for her rough arms and boyish hair.
Body and soul were wasted on me, she claimed.

Once I had her, boyish, rough,
she abandoned me. Body, soul: these were two continents
of genius she claimed were wasted on me.
Artists will prefer the second and they will be right.

But of these two continents—body, soul—I prefer the first
perhaps with more enthusiasm than wisdom.
Artists will prefer the second and they will be right.
This is what I think: if I could I'd be another

man, one with more enthusiasm than wisdom.
Soldier, coachman, wrestler—even a market bull!
This is what I think. I want to be another thing entirely
for whom there are less infinite ways to be moved.

The girl soldiers on after the boy who runs like a bull.
Far off is snappish, eagle-eyed Love. Flight continues life.
There are less infinite ways to be moved. *Voila!* I write. *Un tableau!*
The body in action is the best picture of the human soul.

Notes

What Was There to Bring Me...: Title comes from a line in St. Augustine's *Confessions.*

Anniversary Song: A bride's response to Angela Sorby's poem, "Museum Piece."

Wood/Cut: Section titles come from the four types of woodcuts traditionally printed by Japanese artists.

Epithalamium

A Commission/ Noel Hallé: Born in Paris 1711, son and scholar of the painter Claude Guy Hallé. Member and eventual head of the Academy, he was made the sub-inspector of the tapestry manufactory of the Gobelins in 1775. Known as a history painter, though considered a better draughtsman than artist. Famous works include "St. Vincent de Paul Preaching," "Autumn," and "The Genii of Poetry, History, Physic and Astronomy." The painting "Atalanta and Hippomenes" was never made into a tapestry. The art critic and philosopher Denis Diderot generally disliked everything he did except for the tapestry cartoon of Atalanta and Hippomenes. Died in 1781.

A Love Story: The lines in quotation marks and italics in the poem on the left hand side of the page are adapted from Charles Swinburne's play in verse, *Atalanta at Caledon.*

The End: Lions were, in mythology, considered sexless. When Atalanta and Hippomenes made love in Venus' temple, her punishment was considered ironic, since, as lions, they would never be able to consummate their passion for each other again. As lions, they were assigned to draw Cybele's chariot.

The Critic: Italicized lines in second stanza and lines "artists will prefer the second and they will be right," "the composition goes straight to my soul," and "the body in action is the best picture of the human soul" adapted from Diderot's criticism.

Acknowledgments

Crazyhorse: "25% Pressure."

Feminist Studies: "Six Girls Without Pants."

The Indiana Review: "What Was There to Bring Me to Delight But to Love and Be Loved," and "Wood/Cut: Two Japanese Prints."

Pleiades: "Parable"

Poetry Northwest: "Stupid."

River City: "Anniversary Song," "Race: A Medley," "Figure Drawing 8," and "Figure Drawing 4."

Willow Springs: "*Scientific American* and St. Theresa" and "Caravaggio, My Left Breast, and The Time My Mother Took a Wrong Turn..."

"Stupid," "25% Pressure," Anniversary Song," and "Death and the Maiden" also appeared in *The New Asian American Poets*, ed. Victoria Chang, University of Illinois Press, 2003.

Thanks to the Wyoming Arts Council, the University of Wyoming, David Baker, Susan Brown, Cathy Carlisi, Eric Heimann, Christopher Howell, Scott Poole and Joelean Copeland for support while writing this book.